NO LONGER
WALKING
DEAD

A Guide to
Overcoming Depression

by

Lareesa Fonville

♥

ISBN: 978-0-9985185-1-0

This book is dedicated to everyone that's in the fight of their lives.

No matter what it looks like, WE WIN in the end!

CONTENTS

INTRODUCTION

"You are not in this alone."

DEPRESSION IS A THIEF. It robs you of time. It steals your joy. It leaves you feeling hopeless and in despair. But, most thieves wreak havoc in your life at night. Depression doesn't wait for night to fall. Oftentimes, it's there at dawn greeting you when you open your eyes. The first thing you see before getting out of bed. The first thing you hear, more annoying than any alarm clock. Yes, it talks. It speaks to you in your own voice so you'll listen. It becomes familiar like a friend, only there are no benefits. Families are drawn apart, relationships crumble, careers come crashing down, weight goes from one extreme to the other, and you feel like nobody understands. But, you are not in this alone and you can get everything back that the enemy stole from you. This disease could've killed you, but you're here. We are here. Our story isn't over yet.

The purpose of this book is to share my story, my battle with depression. I hope it will help someone to realize that they are not alone. That someone understands what you're going through. More importantly, I want you to know that even when you feel like there is no one to turn to, you can always turn to God. It's not easy facing your demons and fighting your past. It's not easy living life when negative thoughts come to steer you away from your destiny. It's not easy dealing with disappointments and failures that almost send you over the edge. The road to overcoming depression isn't going to be easy. But, I'm here to tell you that you can make it. This is a process. One that may even cause you more pain, at least initially. You're going to have to be truthful about what you want and what you don't want, even if it's not "the norm." You're going to have get to the root of the problem. You're going to have to make some tough decisions. You're going to have to take action. You're going to have to become your own accountability partner. You are going to have to become your loudest cheerleader. You are going to have to become your own best friend. You are going to have to start taking care of your mental health. But, that also means you're also going to have to care greatly for your physical and spiritual health. It all goes hand in hand. I know this seems like a lot, but balance is what we are seeking to achieve.

Right now, at this very moment, you get to decide how you are going to live your life. Think about what you want to have in this moment. Do you want more joy? Do you want more peace? What about more happiness? You can have it. Don't listen to the part of you that's saying you can't. You can. Whatever it is that you want, believe me when I say, you can have it. It may not seem like it right now, but you can. Life will get better, and guess what? Through this process, you will learn that God has always loved you and He always will. Even though you've felt all alone, God has never left or forsaken you.

"Be strong and courageous. Do not be afraid or terrified because of them, for the LORD your God goes with you; he will never leave you nor forsake you."

Deuteronomy 31:6

The Bible tells us in Deuteronomy 31:6 that the Lord will never leave or forsake us. Even when we've left Him, He is still there loving us, caring for us, and strengthening us. As you read these pages, remember you are not alone. You've never been alone. I know what you're going through and the tough road you are about to embark on. Overcoming depression is far from being easy. Some people don't make it out alive. But, you will. I believe that you will overcome this and live a long, happy, satisfying, purpose-filled life. Do you believe it? Don't worry, you don't have to have a lot of faith. Just a little is all it takes. But, getting better is going to require you to make a lifelong commitment to yourself. Can you do that? Of course, you can. Will you do that? Hmmm, now that's the question. Will you allow yourself the opportunity to live your best life from this day forward? Will you let go of everything that's holding your emotions in bondage? Will you fight for your sanity? Will you be truthful with yourself? Will you take the necessary steps to make life fuller? Will you allow yourself to heal? Will you permit yourself to grow? If you are ready to commit to yourself, keep reading.

CHAPTER ONE

DEPRESSION IS A SERIOUS CONDITION THAT SHOULDN'T BE TAKEN LIGHTLY. Some people think depression is a weakness and they can get stronger on their own. But, help is needed. There are varying degrees, but in every case, the root of the problem needs to be addressed. You can't just snap out of it, like some people that obviously don't have an empathetic bone in their body, will tell you. Trying to "snap out of it" can cause things to spiral out of control and cause suicidal thoughts. If those feelings are left alone, it can cause a person to act on those thoughts.

Let's be clear. I am not a doctor and I'm surely no expert on depression. However, I've lived my life fighting through years of pain, trying to see through tear stained lenses. I have faked enough smiles and laughs to last me a lifetime. I've cried myself to sleep more times than I can count. I've struggled with why I should even get out of bed in the mornings. I've pictured what life would be like without me here. I've pretended to love life in public and, at times, hated my very existence behind closed doors.

Attacks are real. Anything can trigger an episode. Anything can, from a memory, a song, a comment, or, even an unkind facial expression. Anything can send you to that dark place and IF you don't recognize it and choke the life out of it, it can choke the life out of you. If you let it linger and fester in your mind, it's harder and harder to get out. It's almost like a mouse trapped in a maze. There is a way out; you just have to find it. You just have to keep walking through life. Don't let the walls cave in on you. You have to breathe, knowing that everything will be alright. Stay calm, even when you can't see the how, when, or know why this is happening to you.

Let's take a moment right now to decompress. I want you to do something very simple. I want you to breathe. I know what you're thinking. You're already breathing. Yes, yes, I know. But, I want you to focus on your breathing. It's been proven that simple breathing techniques can help you de-stress, relieve anxiety, and promote relaxation. So, take a minute to do this. It doesn't matter if you're sitting up or laying down. Breathe through your nose only, and inhale for a count of four. Then, exhale for a count of four. Do that again. Inhale, counting to four. Exhale, counting to four. Isn't that calming? It's simple, too, right? Breathing only through your nose is said to add a natural resistance which calms the nervous system and reduces stress. You can do this anytime of the day. When life tries to overwhelm you, just take a moment to breathe, ok?

Now, I'm not going to assume that I know what you're going through. It would be naïve of me to think that. Everyone and every situation is different. There is nothing new under the sun. But, to you, it may feel like you're the only one in the world going through your situation. In fact, that's what the enemy wants you to think. His job is to kill, steal, and destroy. A lot of times, he will start with your dreams, hopes, and aspirations. We get tricked into thinking we are hopeless or our situation is hopeless. But, that's simply not true.

Right now, you may feel like you are the walking dead, just going through the motions of life. Do you feel numb or stuck sometimes? A lot of people feel this way.

For me, it was far greater than just feeling sad for a short period. Everyone gets sad from time to time. But, for some of us, we get caught in a prolonged period of sadness that makes it difficult to make decisions, causes us to be unproductive, worry, or can have us feeling hopeless.

"The thief cometh not, but for to steal, and to kill, and to destroy: I am come that they might have life, and that they might have it more abundantly."

John 10:10

The Bible tells us in John 10:10, that Jesus came that we might have life and that we might have it more abundantly. I believe that. I also believe that depression and an abundant life doesn't mix. Walking around in a daze is not what He wants for our lives. We are the apple of His eye and He loves us so very much. We are important to God and He wants us to have peace and joy. Perhaps, in your darkest moments you've had questions like these:

- Am I important to God?

- I've prayed, why isn't He answering?

- Why do I feel this way?

- How do I get peace and joy?

- If we want it and He wants to give it to us, why don't we already have it?

I want to step back a moment. Just like I can't assume to know your situation, I can't assume that everyone reading this book is a Christian. So, if you are not certain that you are in a position to receive what God has for you, I want you to do the following: Ask God right now to forgive you of your sins and ask Jesus Christ to come into your heart. Romans 10:9 says, "If you declare with your mouth, "Jesus is Lord," and believe in your heart that God raised him from the dead, you will be saved." I know it sounds super simple, but that's because it is. People make it confusing and hard by adding all their opinions and doctrines, but all God want us to do is confess and believe. If you just did, congratulations! The

Angels in Heaven are rejoicing and so am I! Make sure you also ask Him to fill you with His Holy Spirit. It's His Spirit that will comfort you, keep you, teach you, and guide you.

But, what if you're already a Christian and you're depressed? That was my situation and it caused me to doubt my faith a little bit. No, let me be all the way real. It caused me to doubt a lot! I mean, I loved the Lord. But, how could I love the Lord with all my heart and not love the life He gave me? How can I say I have faith when I can't seem to get out and *stay out* of deep episodes of depression? This is where I had to do some soul searching and ask God for help. A patty-cake surface prayer wasn't going to help me. I needed some real help. I was tired of having a wet face and not know I was crying, or sometimes even why I was crying. I was tired of shutting people out, not returning phone calls, or showing up to events. I can't recall how many times I'd pretended to be sick, when it was life that I was really sick of. Why was I feeling this way? Why am I going through this?

I needed answers. So, I went to the only place

that has an answer for everything. I went to the Word. I didn't need a preacher, televangelist, or inspirational social media post. I didn't need a prophetic word or anyone laying hands on me. I needed an open Bible. I needed to dig deep. I needed revelation. I needed God to show me that I wasn't alone in this and that I could overcome this feeling of depression. I needed that peace and joy that I longed for. The peace and joy He said was mine and let me tell you, when you start looking for God, He shows up!

Did you know that many people of faith have experienced depression in their lifetimes? One is David, remember the Bible story of him? David made terrible, terrible decisions and as a result, he didn't have an easy life. Sound familiar? A lot of what we're going through is because we made a stupid mistake or two somewhere. We start beating ourselves up to the point where we are just beat. But, if you take time to really examine David's story, you'll realize that even Kings get caught up and get depressed. But, just like David, we are not out of the Lord's will just because we are hurting. People will have us believing that nonsense. God will always love us. There is nothing we can do that will take away His love for us. Nothing. Sometimes, we think God is punishing us or has forgotten about us, but that couldn't be farther from the truth.

David wasn't the only one depressed back in the day. Remember Job? He lost everything. I mean literally everything. He lost his sheep, oxen, and camels. That's like losing your job and all the money in your bank account. He no longer had a way to provide. But, he didn't just lose his possessions. He lost his servants, his sons and daughters. He lost the people that were around him and close to him. Perhaps you've lost a job and took a loss from a venture that didn't pan out. Perhaps, you've lost loved ones, too. It may feel like you've lost everything, just like Job. Sometimes, its so hard to bear the weight of loss. Job's weight was so great that he began to question why he was ever born in the first place. Have you ever been that close to the edge? I have. I've gone to the edge with pills, knives, and even a gun. But, God!!!

Moses is another example. He was depressed because he was betrayed by his own people. I'm sure we've all experienced betrayal from friends and family members that we've done so much for. Jeremiah was rejected, poor, and wrestled with loneliness. He, too, wondered why he was ever born. Take some time and read the stories of Naomi, Hannah, Saul, Nehemiah, and many others. For thousands of years, depression has been prevalent. This isn't something new that you're going through. When you start reading, you'll notice the Bible doesn't use the word "depression." It uses similar words, such as "downcast," "brokenhearted," "troubled," "miserable," "despairing," and "mourning," among others. But, it's all the same. Just different words to describe emotional pain. You'll also see, there were people from all walks of life who struggle, just like you.

Another person who experienced depression was Elijah. He, too, didn't want to live anymore because he was so discouraged with life. He was a mighty man of God who'd experience many victories, yet he had such thoughts. I'm sure you can recall many successful things you've accomplished in your life, but perhaps the only thoughts that come mostly to mind are the failures, am I right? At least that what it was like for me. I bypassed the triumphs quickly, yet I dwelled on my shortcomings far too much and for far too long. The healing process began when I had to answer the question I'm about to ask you.

Why are you depressed?

You may not be able to answer that right now. I couldn't for the longest. I didn't know why and I was embarrassed because I didn't have an answer. People would ask me, "What's wrong?" and I didn't know. Life was good. I couldn't find a real reason to account for why I was acting the way I was. I didn't have an answer because I was only looking for a surface truth. This answer goes way beyond the surface. I'll ask you again.

Why are YOU depressed?

Did your marriage fail? Did you lose your job? Did you lose a dear friend? Did a loved one pass away? Are you unhappy with the way you look? Do you keep failing at something? What is it? Why are YOU depressed? If one or all of those things happened, that still wouldn't be an answer. Those are situational things that happen in life. Those things can happen to anyone. Why are some people depressed and some people aren't? There has to be something deeper. A deeper reason as to why we react to situations in a manner that isn't healthy mentally, physically, or spiritually.

To find the true answer, we must go deeper. When situations happen, are you upset with yourself, someone else, or God? I want you to really think about this question. Be truthful with yourself. Freedom from years of pain lies within the truth of your answer. This, my friend, is where healing begins. Where are you placing blame?

When situations happen, are you upset with yourself, someone else, or God?

Someone else: Granted, some of the situations we've found ourselves in are because of the actions of other people. But, most of the time, we exaggerate their participation to continue to displace blame. Yes, people have hurt us and will hurt us, but we are responsible for how much of that hurt we allow. Many times, we hold onto hurts much longer than we should. We not only need to forgive them, but we also need to forgive ourselves for allowing them to hurt us. We spend days, weeks, even years harboring resentment. Let it go. I'm serious, let it go! If we are truly being honest with ourselves, each one of us has played a much larger part in our suffererings that we'd probably care to admit. When we blame others, it says a lot about how we see ourselves. We can see flaws in others, but not in ourselves. You're subconsciously saying, it's ok for others to make mistakes, but you can't. That's an unrealistic demand for perfection and it puts way too much pressure on you. This doesn't mean that you can't rate the actions of others and treat them accordingly. But, you can't shift responsibility. This is your life. Stop blaming people for the things that happen to you. It's time to take personal responsibility for your happiness.

God: Some of us are quick to blame God for all the bad things that happen in our lives. When in fact, most of the things that happen to us are of our own doings. We just fail to see that our past decisions and actions have allowed our present circumstances to be what they are. There will always be good and bad, right and wrong, light and darkness. That's the way our world works. There can be no rainbow without rain. So, thinking that our lives will only be sunshine and happiness is foolish. We have to take responsibility, not only for our actions, but also for our reactions. If you are one that blames God, you've made Him a victim when He's already made you victorious. It is said, "The truth will set you free." But, most people don't want to know the truth. They'll happily live in a lie, as long as it feels good. We don't want the responsibility of looking inward. It's easier to blame someone you can't see. It's easier to blame someone superhuman. It's easier to hate someone that isn't your reflection in the mirror. It's easier to blame God than to actually believe we are part of the problem. But, can we be honest here? Some peope create their own storms and then get upset when it rains. But, why does God's reputation have to be on the line every time something bad happens? A lot of us seem to be blind and can't see the relationship between what has happened to us and our actions. Poor God! He gets blamed, when we are really to blame due to bad decisions, foolishness, mistakes, or sins. Let's go back to Job. When Job was going though all he went through, he didn't blame God once. You would think with all those trials and tribulations that he would have. But, he didn't. We have to learn to be more like Job. Never once did God promise that we would never suffer in this life. I honestly believe that a lot of what we go through is to bring us closer to Him, not farther away. Instead of looking for excuses to blame Him, we should be trusting Him. I know it's hard to do when you're going through adversities. But, I strongly suggest you stop blaming God and ask for His help. When we stop blaming Him, we can see His beauty, our beauty, and the beautiful world we live in.

Yourself: Anyone who has ever felt depressed can tell you that feeling of self-blame and guilt can be a bit overwhelming. We are going to talk more about this in Chapter 3, but this is the reason I was in such a dark place for so long. I blamed myself for everything. Any and every thing was always my fault, even if I verbally placed the blame on someone else. Internally, it was my fault. In my head, it was my fault. If I failed at something, I considered myself a total failure. In my mind, I couldn't do anything right. I was extremely critical of myself, but I gave everyone around me free passes. I was quick to forgive others, but couldn't seem to do the same for myself. The questions that I'm asking you, I asked myself. The process that I'm taking you through, I've been through myself. This has been quite a journey and a learning process. I've learned that self-blame is one of the most toxic forms of emotional abuse. When I used to think of emotional abuse, I never thought that abuse could be coming from myself. But, it sure can. Even if we blame God or someone else, truth is, the responsibility is with <u>us</u> and always has been. We may just not be at a point of taking responsibility yet.

Like I said, we are going to talk more about this in Chapter 3. But, now that we know we are really blaming ourselves, we now have to stop doing it. I know, I know, it's not going to be easy. But, your sanity is worth going through the process. Your happiness is waiting on you to go through the process. We need to replace old, destructive thinking and habits with new and productive ones. We are going to overcome!

As you continue reading, I want you to remember there is hope. Each step that I urge you to take is to help you. It's what's helped me. Do I still battle? Yes, at times, I do. But, it is my hope that we can take these steps daily together, knowing we aren't fighting this battle alone.

CHAPTER TWO

TALK TO SOMEONE. Reaching out isn't a sign of weakness, it's a sign of strength. However, the very nature of this disease makes it difficult to reach out for help. Lonliness and isolating yourself makes what you're feeling worse. I just hope you don't make the same mistake that I did. I shared my thoughts with someone who wasn't supportive at all. I'm mostly considered a loner or a very private person. I have a hard time asking people for help. People come to me all the time, but I always talked to food. Yes, food. That was my confidant, my best friend.

I remember a time when I was going through a very difficult time and I just needed an ear. Someone to simply listen that wouldn't judge me. I chose the wrong person. They wouldn't stop asking questions and analyzing everything I said. I wasn't asking them to solve my problem. I only needed a listening ear. Someone to be there. Someone to care. But then, they went on and on about what was going on with them and throwing out random suggestions to "fix" my situation. What they went through had nothing to do with what I was going through. All I could think was, "why did I call them?" It bugs me when people listen with the intent to speak instead of listening with the intent of, get this, listening! Why do people feel like that they need to offer advice or give you suggestions as to what you should do? The thing about me is this: when I need your advice, I'll ask for it. Until then, close your mouth and try to be supportive.

The good news is, I didn't let that incident deter me from finding a real listening ear. I suggest you turn to trusted friends and family members. The keyword here is trusted. Even if you've distanced yourself from them in the past, reach out. I had a hard time with this because I'd been in isolation for so long. Depression can really kill relationships. The other person may not even know what happened. You started calling less and less, stopped attending events, let their calls go to voicemail, texts go unanswered. Until one day, they just looked up and you were nowhere to be found. I know you preferred it this way while you tried to sort out your feelings about how life got so out of control. But, real friends and real family don't just disappear. I'm sure you have people that love and care for you. These treasured relationships could be the very thing that helps you through this rough patch. Reach out.

Also, try joining a support group. Believe it or not, many people are going through the same thing you are. According to current national statistics, there are approximately 19 million Americans living with depression. In fact, it affects so many people that it has been referred to as the "common cold" of mental illness. I know you probably don't like the term, mental illness. I don't, but we have to be honest with what we are dealing with. Whatever you believe, if you are dealing with depression, your life is being attacked through the crevices of your mind. Even though you may feel alone, you aren't. Of those 19 million people, I'm sure most will never attend a group meeting. It's likely that they are too ashamed or embarrassed to admit publicly there is a problem. I was embarrassed for a long time. I didn't want someone putting a label on me. But, for me, telling people became my way of truly being in the healing process. When you are embarrassed or ashamed of something enough to hide it, it has a hold on you. Have you ever heard that the first step is admitting you have a problem? Well, that's what I had to do. I had to acknowledge that I wasn't in control of my emotions. I had to do that in order to gain control. Does that make sense? It was a step I needed to take and one you should consider taking as well. That's also a part of taking responsibility.

There are more women than men in these support groups. I believe that's because men believe they must be strong at all times, so they tend to be in denial. But, in these groups, you'll be able to share your experiences and encourage each other. There are several online you can participate in until you are ready to share face to face. They all should be free, confidential, and not require you to sign up in advance. Sometimes, the first meeting can feel awkward, but give it a few times before you decide to just give up. Whatever route you choose, make sure you begin to open up and talk about your feelings. The more you listen to others and how they've dealt with certain situations, you'll feel more comfortable sharing. Give it time. Hopefully, one day your story will help someone else.

If you're not at the place where you feel open to sharing within a group, there are several people that get paid to listen, too. They even offer a nice couch for you to sit or lie down on while you're disclosing your inner most thoughts. If we're going to share, we might as well be comfy, right? Some are licensed, some are not, so do your research. Even those that are licensed may not be a practitioner, who can offer prescribed treatments. But, be careful of those who are quick to medicate you. I've been to a couple of doctors who were swift putting their pens to prescription pads. I'm not saying medications aren't necessary at times, but everyone who is going through depression does not need a prescription. Drugs don't correct the underlying problem. They only make life a little more tolerable. Depending on your definition of tolerable, of course. A lot of these so-called treatments can often cause "crazy" symptoms, like mood swings and suicidal thoughts. I thought the point of getting help was so we wouldn't kill ourselves. Hmmm, just be careful. You have something inside you that <u>only you</u> can give the world. We need you here. We need you to get better. We need you to survive.

CHAPTER THREE

YOU ARE NOT TO BLAME. Earlier, we became aware that we must take responsibility for our lives. We can't blame God. We can't blame others. We can't blame anyone, not even ourselves. Mistakes happen. Life happens. We are human. The choices we've made are just that ... choices. You can't change the past. You can only move on from here by taking full responsibility for your life.

It's never too late to be what you were meant to be. Take one day, one step at a time to change behaviors. We do better, most times, when we know better. Hopefully, the words within these pages are going to help you see yourself. Truly see yourself. Not the self you portray to the world. The real you that has been hiding underneath negative feelings for much too long. But, right now, I don't want you to think of those negative feelings. I don't want you to think about your past. I don't even want you to think of your present. I want you to take a a few minutes right now to look into your future.

Go get a piece of paper and a pen. If you don't have any paper close by, I'll include a couple of blank pages for you to write on just a few sentences down. Now, this might sound a little weird, but I want you to write down your perfect day. From when you'll wake up and open your eyes, to the time you'll fall asleep. Where are you? What is around you? Who are you with? What are you doing? Close your eyes for a moment and think about it. Breathe deeply and let your mind roam into your future. Now, write it all down. Every detail of what you just envisioned. If you feel like you missed something, close your eyes again and revisit that image in your mind. See it clearly until you can hear the sounds and smells as well. Let your senses become engaged with what you want for your life. Allow those positive vibes to flow out into the universe. I know it's not easy and I'm not asking you to be a writer, but try to capture what you saw on paper. Then, once you're finished, post it on a wall or mirror, somewhere where you will see it every day.

As promised, here's some space for you to jot down your thoughts:

_____

_____

_____

_____

_____

_____

_____

_____

_____

_____

_____

_____

_____

_____

_____

_____

_____

_____

_____

_____

_____

_____

_____

_____

_____

_____

_____

_____

_____

_____

_____

_____

_____

_____

_____

_____

_____

_____

_____

_____

_____

_____

_____

_____

_____

_____

_____

_____

_____

_____

_____

_____

_____

Now, that we know what we want, we must take the necessary steps to get there. Say this serenity prayer with me: "God grant me the serenity to accept the things I cannot change; the courage to change the things I can; and the wisdom to know the difference. Amen." This prayer has helped millions overcome addictions around the globe. It can also help us overcome depression. In fact, many depressed people have turned to alcohol, drugs, sex, food, or many other things to cope. But, it doesn't work. These types of things just make things worse. That's why we need God to help us accept the things we can't change. It's a waste of energy trying to control something that is outside of our control. It only leaves you frustrated and sad. The serenity prayer helps us find our inner strength and allows us to shift our thoughts. We can concentrate on the things we can change and develop faith to improve our situations.

This journey of overcoming depression takes courage. I applaud each person reading this book for taking the steps to escape the misery of depression. You can make good decisions. You have the ability to control your emotions. You have the power to transform your life.

CHAPTER FOUR

D REAM AGAIN. Did you like the "perfect day" exercise in the last chapter? I have to admit, I didn't when I first did it. But, it helped to write out exactly what I wanted and to see it every day. Now, I don't want you to think about just one day. I want you to think about what you really want out of life. Where do you see yourself five, ten, twenty years from now?

For some, thinking about the future causes extreme anxiety. They are either afraid of success or afraid of failure, and choose to stay stagnant in the "safe" place they are in. Only that safe place isn't safe, not mentally and oftentimes, physically as well. I believe it's because we tend to sometimes place these high standards on ourselves. Or, we've adopted a standard someone else may have placed on us. It's a terrible feeling to have to measure your life by unrealistic standards. Many of us have a fantasy in our heads of how life is supposed to be, but fail to take the necessary steps to actually obtain that life.

I have a vision board in my room. It is on the wall beside my bed. I see it every morning when I wake up. I didn't always have one. But, now I know how important it is to dream. I know how important it is to hope for more. Hope will cause you to live. Hope is the expectation of a positive outcome. Hope wants something to become true or to happen in your life. We can never give up hope. If we don't have hope, we have nothing to hold onto.

Create a vision board. If you've already done one, do it again. Mine is very basic. It is on black poster board with different pictures and sayings from magazines. I cut them out and made a collage. Every aspect of my life is on my vision board. From spirituality, to my love life, to family, career paths, to my hobbies, to places I want to visit, etc. The basics of my dreams are on that board. It's funny, as I'm typing this, I can look over at it and in the corner, I see a woman with curly hair. She has a beautiful flower in her hair. I just realized that vision just came true last month. The first time I'd ever worn a flower in my hair was at a convention in Texas a few weeks ago. I know what you're thinking, what's so grand about wearing a flower in your hair? It's not the flower. It's what the flower represents *to me*. I posted the picture because the image was so carefree. I wanted to be that woman who didn't have a care in the world. The moment I wore that flower, I didn't. I was free in so many ways. As I continue to look at that board, I'm noticing that so many of my dreams have been realized. I've traveled to other countries, I've helped hundreds of people. I've crossed off several goals and bucket list items. You know what? I'm going to dream again with you. I'm going to redo my vision board. This time, I'm going all out. Let's really dream. What do you want? I mean, really want? What are the things that you want so badly it scares you? The things you are afraid to tell other people about? The things that require much more responsibility than you currently desire to undertake because depression has left you drained? What do you want so bad you can taste it? What are the things that keep you up at night? What slipped away from you? What did you let go of, but it never let go of you? I want those things on the board. If you can't find magazine clippings, just write them down for now. But, get your dream board together.

Remember, how I didn't notice I'd accomplished so many things? I think that's what happens to a lot of us. We fail to take notice of how awesome we truly are. Life has us pulled in so many directions that we are on to the next project before we even celebrate or even recognize what we've accomplished. This is going to be important as we move forward. Taking the time to acknowledge small successes will help keep us motivated and energized. There are some I would imagine that would disagree with this strategy of action. But, for those of us who are extremely critical of ourselves, every win should be celebrated. I'm not talking about throwing a party every time you complete a task. But, we need to know it's ok to feel joy and satisfaction when a goal is completed, no matter how small. I believe this will increase positive emotions such as confidence, happiness, and self-respect. I suggest creating memories around the most important successes in your life. For example, create a success jar. Put all your achievements on little pieces of colored paper throughout the year. So, in the future, when we are doubting our abilities or feeling overwhelmed, we will remember what we've accomplished, how far we've come, or what we can do when we set our minds to it. Like me, most depressives dwell on what we didn't achieve. Let's shift our thinking and recognize the value of what we did achieve! It's not about the celebration, its about growing and creating your best life. Let today be the day you give up who you've been for who you can become.

CHAPTER FIVE

G ET OUT OF THE HOUSE. Depending on what type of depression you have, you may find it extremely hard to get out of bed or off the couch. You may only socialize with people when you have to, like at work or at church. The other times, you're home. Sometimes, you even call yourself a "homebody," and that may be true to a certain extent. But, if you're ALWAYS at home, let's face facts, you're hiding. I know firsthand about hiding. I didn't go to my mailbox reguarly. If someone showed up at my door, I wouldn't answer. Fast food delivery drivers only knew me by an arm out the door. I didn't want to be seen, by anyone. I only went to the grocery store if I had to and while I was there I stocked up to make sure it would be awhile before I had to go again. I opted to go to smaller stores than major ones, knowing that my chances of being seen were less. Of course, my options for healthier choices were also lessened and junk food crept in at every trip. I even started shopping online for the smallest of items, even though I'm not even five minutes from a shopping center. I made sure I didn't have to sign for anything, making sure all packages could be left on the porch. I'd peep out of the window to make sure my neighbors were out of sight before opening the door. I even waited until it was dark to feed or walk my dog.

I didn't enjoy being in solitude, but home was the only place I didn't have to pretend. My cream-colored walls didn't judge me. They didn't criticize me. They didn't look at me weird. They didn't ask me how tall I was. They didn't ask me if I still had my businesses. They didn't ask me how much weight I'd lost. They didn't ask me if I was still married. They didn't ask me if I had children. They didn't ask me how I was doing, and therefore, I didn't have to lie and say, "I'm good." I told myself that I was just speaking it into existence. You know, "calling those things which be not as though they were" as mentioned in Romans 4:17. However, saying 'I'm good' was the biggest lie that I told myself." I call myself a person of integrity. I truly strive to be honest, yet I can't answer a question as simple as, "How are you?"

"Saying 'I'm good' was the biggest lie that I told myself."

I was lying to myself every time I parted my lips to say those words. Those two words covered up the hurt and the pain just long enough for me to get back to the comfort of the walls. All I really wanted back then was for someone, anyone, to say, "No, you're not."

But, those words never came and I spent years in a daze. I call it walking dead. I was still functioning in society, but not connecting to people and actively engaging in life. Some days were darker than others and its purely by the grace of God that I am still here. The same may be true for you, I don't know. Everybody deals with things differently. But, I do know that it's also by God's grace that you are still here, too.

Where I went wrong, is that I allowed the isolation to continue. That prolonged what I was going through. I didn't want to be around other people, but I *needed* to be around other people. I needed to reconnect with life. It's hard at first. All I could do initially was stand in the window and let the sunlight shine on my face. It helped. Then, I was able shower and get dressed. Then, I was able to actually step outside and sit on my front porch. Then, a walk around the block. Then a trip to a bookstore. Baby steps. It's ok to take baby steps. It's even ok if we take a step and fall. What's not ok is when we stay down. We must get up every, single time we fall. No matter how hard it is. Every time, get up.

You can choose where you want to go. The goal here is to just change your environment and don't let yourself become isolated. You can get a grip on this. I know you can. If you find it difficult, set a schedule and stick to it. For example, if you have an old friend you'd like to reconnect with, schedule an activity with them. Make it fun. This is not a meeting to dredge up the past. This is to reconnect with someone supportive. If you both like to workout, a trip to the gym would be great for more reasons than one! Just do it. Soon the difficult things won't be so difficult. Social contact is necessary. It may bring anxiety initially, but it won't worsen the depression. It will help, trust me.

Do things that make you feel good. Don't sit around doing nothing. That will more than likely cause you to think negatively. Move around. Get your blood flowing. The only way to beat this is to take action. I know, I know. It's the hardest thing to do when you feel completely and utterly exhausted by life, but you must. If you can't get out of the house, open a window to at least get some fresh air. Or, call someone. It will help improve your outlook and hopefully, your mood. Do you have a pet? Pets can make you feel less isolated and get you out of the house as well. They also give you a sense of being needed and can bring a lot of joy to your life.

Here are a few more tips:

- Go see a clergy member or teacher
- Workout with a friend
- Help someone else by volunteering
- Have lunch or coffee with a friend
- Go to the movies or a concert
- Take a day trip to a park or museum
- Go for a walk with a workout buddy
- Take a new class
- Find a new hobby or join a creative club
- Go see a mentor

These things help tremendously. Make sure you expose yourself to a little sunlight every day. It will boost your mood. Try to aim for at least 15-20 minutes a day.

Also, try to get some exercise in. When you exercise, endorphins are released that help you feel good. Staying active will allow you to focus on other things.

Make sure you are getting enough sleep. A lot of mood issues develop because of sleeping problems. Everyone is different, but try to aim for six to eight hours of sleep each night. I know that's easier said than done when you're suffering with depression. But, there is a definite link between lack of sleep and how it affects your mental and physical health. On the other hand, some people oversleep when they are overwhelmed. They are tired all the time and all they want to do is sleep. They have an "I don't care" attitude. That was me. I didn't have any energy and I lacked the motivation to sometimes, get out of bed. When you're asleep, there is a break from the pain. You get a chance to check out and stop thinking. The world pauses, but not really. All you managed to do was let life go on without you, without actually letting it go on without you. I read somewhere that 80 percent of people have problems sleeping. Wow, that's a lot of people. For me, I had to put myself on a routine. I set an alarm to tell me when it was time for bed and I started getting myself up at the same time every morning. When I didn't feel like getting out of bed, I made myself do it anyway. If you have problems getting to sleep or oversleeping, share this with your doctor. They can provide you with solutions which may prove to be helpful to your specific situation.

Eat healthy. I can't stress this enough. I'm an emotional eater, so when I'm depressed I eat. Oftentimes, it's junk, junk, and more junk which causes increased mood swings. This is like trying to heal yourself with poison. Make sure you are eating good foods that are nutrient rich. I suggest lean proteins, leafy green vegetables, fruits, and whole grains. Limit sugars, processed foods, and alcohol consumption. Everything in moderation.

Find a new passion. When we discussed vision boards, did you really think about what you wanted to do? Do you like your current job? If not, take the steps to get a new one. If you aren't in a position to get a new one, find a new passion. What do you care deeply about? For me, my love of writing helped me feel like I had more purpose in life. It gave me an outlet to share my testimony, hopefully helping others going through the same challenges.

They say, "Before you can see the light, you have to deal with the darkness." Deal with it, day by day. Sometimes, it's moment by moment. But, you are stronger than you think. Oftentimes, people speak about depression like it's something only weak people go through. I disagree. I believe we are strong, loving, caring individuals. Coming out of depression alive is one of the strongest things you can do. I don't know who is reading this book right now. I don't know anything about you. But, I see you. I see you in your future. I see you better. I see you happy. I see you brave. I see you strong. I see you courageous. I see you blessed. I see you shining like a bright star, piercing out from the dark of night. I see you trusting God and His promises, rather than your emotions. I see the overcomer in you. I see you and I hope you will choose to see it, too.

Epilogue

"Now may the God of peace, who through the blood
of the eternal covenant brought back from the dead
our Lord Jesus, that great Shepherd of the sheep,
equip you with everything good for doing his will,
and may he work in us what is pleasing to him,
through Jesus Christ, to whom be glory for ever and
ever. Amen."

Hebrews 13: 20-21

Epilogue

Acknowledgments

Thank you for taking the time to read this book. I pray something I've said has touched your heart. I also pray that you will begin to speak life to your situation and take the necessary steps to take your life back. Clear your mind, give it all to God, and rest well tonight. Tomorrow is a new day! Go LIVE!

About the Author

Lareesa Fonville is an entrepreneur, who currently lives in Chesterfield, Virginia. She is the author of Cyn No More, Arrows: A Collection of Poetry, Reecipe For Success: A Cookbook with A Recipe for Life, Resting Inn Peace, and is currently working on her latest book, The Secret. Lareesa wants to hear from you! She can be contacted via email at support@lareesa.com or online social channels at @lareesainc.

Resources:

- If you are experiencing a medical emergency, dial 9-1-1.

- Suicide Prevention Hotline: 1-800-273-TALK (8255)

- National Alliance on Mental Illness: 1-800-950-NAMI (6264), https://www.nami.org

- Centers for Disease Control and Prevention: Division of Mental Health, 1-800-CDC-INFO (1-800-232-4636), http://www.cdc.gov/mentalhealth

- Depression and Bipolar Support Alliance: 1-800-826-3632, http://www.dbsalliance.org